WHEN THERE IS NO WHY

M.Y. JOURNEE

TABLE OF CONTENTS

Chapter 1 Foundations of Self-Understanding
Nihilism - Life is difficult
Existentialism - Life is not fair
Absurdism - Sometimes There Is No Why
Self-preservationism: Don't have a relationship with someone who doesn't have your best interest at heart

Chapter 2 Navigating Choices and Purpose
Passionism - In life, there are many options; choose one and give it your all
Doism - Just do it
Dogmatism - If there is any doubt, there is no doubt

Chapter 3 Building Resilience and Taking Control
Goodism - Don't engage in any transaction that you didn't initiate
Egoism - You have to always do what is best for you
Realism - Not everyone is going to get on the train
Cynicism - Trust, like the soul, once it is gone, it never returns

Chapter 4 The Importance of Sacrifice and Focus
Asceticism - To achieve anything, you must make sacrifices
Altruism - Don't Let Money or Power Drive Your Pursuits
Optimism - Get busy living or get busy dying
Pragmatism - Live for today with the future in mind
Sameism - Women/men may be different, but we are all the same

Final Reflection - Living with Purpose and Joy
Let's go

WHAT THE HELL

THE UNCHARTED PATH: A LIFE FULL OF ISMS

Rooted entirely in my personal beliefs and experiences, this novella shares the valuable lessons I have learned throughout my life. The key takeaway for you, the reader, is to develop a unique perspective shaped by your personal life journey. Please understand that this novella is not a cure-all or a comprehensive guide for navigating life's complexities. The insights offered here are not intended as philosophical, medical, psychological, or legal advice. They reflect my personal journey, and while you may find similar experiences, your path may differ significantly. The emphasis here is on your ability to cultivate new insights based on your individual experiences.

INTRODUCTION

Have you ever thought, "What the hell?" or doubted your sanity when the world around you feels completely foreign? This realization might strike during a conversation with friends who no longer share your views, in a workplace break room where familiar chatter has turned strained, or even at a social gathering that suddenly feels isolating. Perhaps it's during a heated exchange where you wonder: Am I the only one who hasn't changed?

If you've felt this way, know that you are not alone. Change is a constant presence in our lives, and it's all too easy to feel as if you're being left behind. But let me assure you: it's not you; it's the world around you. Change is not just inevitable; it is an intricate part of our existence. Sometimes, we ride the waves of transformation, unaware of our adaptation, while at other times, we find ourselves standing still, observing the shifting tides. Everything we once knew, the language we spoke, the music that resonated with us, the fashions we wore, and even our work ethics evolved over time.

We often ponder whether we have somehow become outliers in this ongoing evolution. The reality is that change affects us all, both personally and across generations. The "isms" that manifest from our language and values to our worldviews are vivid evidence of this continuous metamorphosis. Every generation seems convinced its way of life is the only viable path, yet the truth remains: every era reshapes the very fabric of culture and society. What feels contemporary now will inevitably become a relic of the past.

This novella contains insights and "isms" that have guided me through life's unpredictable landscape. Some concepts are straightforward and accessible, while others delve into more nuanced psychological perspectives. I have listened to countless narratives from friends and family facing life's daunting challenges—challenges that can often feel insurmountable. In these moments, I have been privileged to share my isms and have consistently witnessed their potential to illuminate paths forward.

This novella serves as my personal compass, designed to help navigate the complexities of existence. Think of it as a map of "isms" meant to ease your journey through both familiar and unexpected obstacles. The teachings presented here are not mere abstractions but lessons forged from my daily experiences. They offer wisdom that can fundamentally shift your perspective, shaping how you approach decisions, relationships, and your role in the world.

As you progress through these pages, you will encounter

various challenges ranging from progress and growth to caution and introspection. These themes are intricately connected, providing a deeper understanding of our world. The isms explore the delicate interplay between tradition and innovation, belief and reality, certainty and ambiguity. They compel us to think critically, reflect introspectively, and engage in open dialogue.

Ultimately, the goal is not to provide clear-cut answers but to spark thought, conversation, and personal reflection. Some of my isms may resonate with you strongly, while others might feel distant or unfamiliar. No matter where you find yourself on your own journey, I hope this novella inspires you to explore, question, and grow. The true strength of an ism lies not in its rigidity but in its ability to provoke dialogue, contemplation, and better decision-making.

So, I invite you to join this conversation. Embrace this journey with an open heart and mind. Challenge your assumptions, and always remember that no single ism has all the answers. Through curiosity and dialogue, we can begin navigating the rich and complex landscape shaped by these ideas. Let's embark on this adventure together.

Definitions

The definitions presented in this novella reflect my personal interpretation of their meaning and may not align perfectly with the traditional uses or definitions of these words. With that in mind, these "isms" refer to distinct philosophies, ideologies, or belief systems that shape how I perceive the world and approach life.

While some isms inspire progress and positivity, others may serve as cautionary tales or restrictive frameworks, depending on the perspective from which they are viewed. Ultimately, they have guided me through life's complexities, shaping decisions, influencing identities, and subtly yet profoundly affecting behaviors.

CHAPTER 1

Existentialism - Life is difficult

Existentialism emphasizes the inherent challenges, struggles, and often absurdity of life. It acknowledges that life can be difficult, uncertain, and filled with suffering. I believe individuals must confront these difficulties and find meaning or purpose despite or perhaps because of the struggle. This philosophy suggests that difficulty is a fundamental part of the human experience, and it is up to each person to navigate it in their own way.

At first glance, this "ism" may seem stark or pessimistic. However, it is one of the most profound truths about the human experience. Acknowledging that difficulty is an inherent part of living, we set ourselves up for resilience, growth, and peace of mind. Accepting that struggle is inevitable allows us to navigate challenges more effectively and to appreciate joy when they appear.

At the age of 14, I received a novella that began with a striking statement: "Life is difficult." At that age, I couldn't fully comprehend this sentiment. However, as I grew older, I came to realize that life is challenging for everyone. Regardless of one's social status, financial situation, health, mental state, or any other positive attribute, the truth remains: "Life is difficult." We all face the realities of life every day, every hour, and every minute. Daily events can significantly impact our lives. Avoiding, ignoring, or trying to escape these challenges will not change the fact that, ultimately, life will continue to be difficult.

Life's challenges take various shapes

External Circumstances: Financial struggles, career setbacks, illness, and loss.
Internal Battles: Self-doubt, anxiety, guilt, and the search for meaning.
Relationships: Navigating miscommunication, heartbreak, and the complexities of nurturing healthy connections.

Accepting Difficulty Is Liberating

Freedom from Unrealistic Expectations: Many people suffer more because they believe life should be easy. When it's not, they feel cheated or defeated.
Strength Through Adversity: Difficult experiences build character, wisdom, and resilience.
Greater Appreciation of Joy: Contrast makes joy sweeter. Understanding difficulty helps us savor moments of ease and happiness.
Empowerment: Accepting life's difficulties encourages problem-solving instead of passive victimhood.

The Silver Lining of Difficulty

Personal Growth: Challenges push us to develop new skills, perspectives, and inner strength.
Connection Through Empathy: Shared struggles forge deeper bonds between people.
Purpose and Meaning: Overcoming obstacles often gives life direction and a sense of accomplishment.

Practical Strategies for Embracing Difficulty

Shift Your Mindset: Instead of asking, "Why me?" ask, "What can I learn from this?"
Focus on What You Can Control: Let go of factors beyond your influence and channel energy into actionable solutions.
Build Resilience: Cultivate mindfulness, gratitude, and regular physical activity to fortify yourself against life's storms.
Seek Support: Don't hesitate to lean on friends, family, or professionals when life feels overwhelming.

Reflection

No one is immune to life's difficulties, regardless of background, status, or achievements. The key is not avoiding them but learning to embrace and navigate them.
Yes, life is difficult, but that's what makes it meaningful. The beauty of life isn't found in a perpetual state of ease but in the strength we develop, the lessons we learn, and the joys we experience despite the challenges. By embracing this "ism," we stop fighting life and start living it fully, scars and all.

Nihilism - Life is Not Fair

Nihilism suggests life lacks inherent meaning, value, or fairness. It asserts that life has no ultimate purpose or objective morality, often highlighting the world's randomness and inherent unfairness. This perspective acknowledges that life may not be "fair" or just, and people must navigate a reality without expecting inherent order or justice.

This philosophy challenges one of our earliest expectations: that fairness, justice, and merit should naturally dictate life outcomes. We are often taught from childhood that good behavior is rewarded and bad behavior is punished. However, the world frequently contradicts this simplistic view, presenting random injustices and unearned privileges.

We have all heard the saying, "That's not fair." To that, I say, really? If you think for a moment that life is fair, I'm sorry to disappoint you. This is a hard truth for some people to accept. Fairness can't exist because, as humans, we have many variables that drive our behavior. You've probably heard the saying, "It's every man/woman for themselves." Life is inherently unfair because we are not robots. We have feelings, needs, desires, and sometimes unresolved traumas. The best candidate isn't always hired; someone may avoid a speeding ticket because they connect with the law enforcement officer, while others get away with breaking the rules simply because. Please don't worry about the fairness of life; it's beyond your control. You cannot control other people's actions, beliefs, or conduct. Once you accept that life is unfair, you will be better prepared to navigate through it.

MY LIFE HAS HAD many instances that demonstrate how unfair it can be. One significant lesson occurred when I was fifteen. I was sitting in my classroom when the principal instructed everyone to pass their school identification to the front of the class. He collected the IDs and left the room. About twenty minutes later, the principal returned and asked me to come with him.

I asked him what I had done wrong when we arrived at his office. He told me that an allegation had been made against me. A fellow student had identified me, based on my school identification photo, as the person who had robbed her the day before. I was shocked and denied any wrongdoing. I asked if he was sure she had said it was me, and he assured me that she had. He mentioned that a witness also identified me as the robber.

I insisted that I wanted to see the accuser in person. When she came into the room, she again identified me as the person who had robbed her. I did not recognize her at all. I repeated that I didn't remember meeting her and maintained my innocence.

A police detective was present and asked the principal to review my conduct record. The principal returned, stating that I had no history of bad behavior and, in fact, was an "A" student. The detective appeared puzzled and then informed the complainant that the matter would have to be resolved in criminal court. At that point, the complainant began to recant her accusation and was subsequently permanently suspended from the school.

I later learned that the witness, a student in my math class, was jealous of my higher grade point average and wanted to have me arrested and expelled. This experience made me realize just how unfair life can be when someone can make false accusations against you simply out of jealousy or personal agenda. This was my first encounter with life's unfairness, but certainly not my last.

The Reality of Life's Unfairness

Unequal Starting Points: Not everyone is born into the same circumstances. Wealth, education, geography, and family support differ widely, affecting opportunities.
Randomness of Events: Illnesses, accidents, and unforeseen hardships can strike without warning, regardless of one's efforts or intentions.
Unrewarded Effort: Hard work doesn't always lead to success; luck or connections sometimes overshadow talent and dedication.

Why This Truth Is Hard to Accept

Humans are inherently wired for fairness. Studies indicate that even young children instinctively expect to be treated equitably. When we encounter personal or societal injustices, we often feel betrayed because it contradicts our understanding of how the world should function.

However, insisting that life must be fair can lead to frustration, resentment, and disillusionment. Accepting life's unfairness does not mean condoning it; instead, it involves learning to navigate wisely within its reality.

Lessons to Learn from Life's Unfairness

Adaptability Over Entitlement: Instead of demanding fairness, focus on adjusting your approach to changing circumstances.
Resilience: Developing mental strength to handle setbacks equips you to keep moving forward, regardless of obstacles.
Empathy for Others: Recognizing the randomness of life

fosters compassion for those who face injustices beyond their control.

Creating Fairness Where Possible: While life may not be inherently fair, individuals can choose to promote fairness in their relationships, workplaces, and communities.

How to Navigate Unfair Situations

Control the Controllable: Focus on what you can change rather than dwelling on external factors.

Reframe Challenges: Unfair experiences often teach resilience, problem-solving, and humility.

Seek Allies: Build networks of support that help level the playing field when life seems stacked against you.

Take Action: Where injustice exists, advocacy and action can create meaningful change.

Examples in Everyday Life

Career: A less qualified colleague may receive a promotion due to favoritism, while your hard work may go unnoticed.

Relationships: Good-hearted people sometimes face betrayals, while manipulative individuals thrive socially.

Health: Some maintain healthy lifestyles yet face chronic illnesses, while others seem untouched by poor habits.

Reflection

Accepting that life is unfair doesn't mean we should yield to injustice; instead, it involves approaching the world with awareness, resilience, and a dedication to finding meaning amid these inequalities.

By embracing this truth, we can concentrate on what truly

matters: living authentically, maximizing our opportunities, and positively impacting the lives of others.

Absurdism - Sometimes there is no "why."

Absurdism suggests that life does not inherently possess meaning or a rational explanation; essentially, there is no clear "why." According to this perspective, seeking meaning or reason in a universe that provides no definitive answers results in an "absurd" condition. In this state, the pursuit of understanding can often feel futile, as events and circumstances may unfold without any deeper explanation.

Sometimes, things simply exist as they are, and there may not always be a reason behind them.
The relentless search for meaning is one of humanity's most fundamental instincts. We are naturally inclined to ask questions, seek causes, and assign reasons to the events and experiences that shape our lives. Yet sometimes, there are no satisfying answers. This concept can initially be unsettling because we crave understanding to maintain control. However, absurdism offers a liberating truth: life doesn't always have to make sense. Accepting this reality can bring a sense of peace amid chaos and ambiguity.

I recall being frequently asked why I chose to attend a particular college. This question arises because my alma mater is not a typical destination for someone who grew up in the inner city. I could not clearly answer "why." I knew nothing about the school, its history, or where it was located. If I had to pick a school that seemed completely inconsistent with my background and knowledge, it would be this one. In

March of my senior year, I was in my guidance counselor's office discussing college applications. When I told her I had not applied to any schools, she was shocked and looked at me in confusion. She got up from her desk, opened her file cabinet, and began searching through college brochures. After several minutes, she said, "We haven't had anyone go to this school in a long time." Then she handed me a brochure that included an application to this school. I took the brochure, reluctantly applied, and was accepted.

In late August, I received a final notice stating that my spot would be given to someone else if I did not acknowledge my acceptance. I had no intention of attending long-term. Three weeks later, I got on a bus and told everyone that I would return in two weeks. Needless to say, I ended up attending for four consecutive years, graduating, and having the best four years of my life. To this day, I cannot explain "why" this set of circumstances occurred. Sometimes I think that I did not really make the decision; rather, the decision was made for me. My takeaway from this and other instances where I cannot find an explanation is that everything happens as it should. I stopped searching for the "why" long ago and now just accept that reality is the only thing that exists. The "why" doesn't require an explanation; it is simply what it is.

Why We Seek a "Why"

Control and Certainty: Knowing "why" something happens gives us a sense of predictability.
Emotional Comfort: Understanding provides closure and validation during difficult times.

Problem-Solving: If we understand the cause, we can fix or avoid similar situations in the future.

When There Is No "Why"

Randomness of Life: Sometimes things happen simply because they do—random accidents, chance encounters, or inexplicable losses.
Complexity Beyond Comprehension: The world is filled with intricate systems whose causes are beyond human understanding.
The Nature of Emotion: Feelings often arise without clear triggers, and searching for a reason only deepens frustration.

The Danger of Forced Meaning

The insistence on finding a "why" can lead to harmful narratives. People may blame themselves unnecessarily, invent convoluted justifications, or cling to false hopes. This mental trap often creates more pain than relief.

Embracing the Absence of "Why"

Mindful Acceptance: Acknowledge that some things are. No reason is required for existence.
Letting go: of the need for constant understanding and freeing yourself from the burden of "what if" thinking.
Living in the Present: Focus on what is rather than endlessly questioning what could have been.

The Power in No "Why"

By accepting that life doesn't always conform to logic or reason, we gain the freedom to experience life as it is, move forward without needing closure, and find beauty in the inexplicable.

Reflection

"Sometimes there is no why, and that is okay." Not everything in life has an explanation, reason, or justification, no matter how much we search for one. The quest for meaning in a universe that provides none can lead to frustration and despair. However, instead of retreating into hopelessness, we can embrace this absurdity directly and live fully in spite of it. Although life may not offer the clear answers we seek, this doesn't diminish its value.

Ultimately, the absence of a clear "why" in life should not lead us to give up; instead, it invites us to fully embrace the present moment. We can live without the need for a definitive purpose or reason and create our own meaning in a world that offers none. In this context, the phrase "sometimes there is no why" reminds us that life's absurdity is not something to fear or avoid but rather something to coexist with—and perhaps even find freedom in.

Self-preservationism - Don't have a relationship with someone who doesn't have your best interest at heart

Self-preservationism involves prioritizing your well-being, mental health, and personal growth by surrounding yourself with people who genuinely support and care for you. It's about making choices that protect your emotional and psychological integrity while maintaining healthy, positive relationships. The essence of this concept is grounded in self-respect, self-preservation, and emotional intelligence.

My first encounter with this issue occurred during my employment. I consistently received excellent performance reviews and spoke to my supervisor about a promotion. When I asked him to recommend me, he responded, "Why do you want to get promoted?" At that moment, I thought, "What does he mean? Why?" I wanted to explain that I was qualified, had worked hard, contributed to the organization's success, and had helped him receive accolades.

Similarly, another supervisor told me that I wouldn't be transferred until he was assigned elsewhere. He didn't want to lose my productivity, as I consistently outperformed the other three employees. Neither supervisor had my best interests in mind; they were solely concerned about their own situations.

Now, consider a friend or partner in a business or personal relationship. If you tell a friend you want to go to college to improve your knowledge and overall life, and they respond, "Why do you want to do that?" or make any derogatory comments, that friend does not have your best interests at heart. They may feel threatened by the prospect of you moving forward and don't want to be left behind. Being involved with someone who does not genuinely care about your well-being is unhealthy. As a result, I have learned to avoid relationships with people who do not have my best interests at heart. A person who truly wants the best for you is someone worth keeping in your life.

Key Aspects

Healthy Boundaries: The importance of establishing boundaries with those who may introduce negativity or harm to your life. If someone consistently overlooks your needs, feelings, or well-being, it is worth evaluating whether they should continue to have a place in your life.

Mutual Respect and Reciprocity: Relationships should be built on mutual respect, where both parties care about and are invested in each other's growth. If a person only takes from the relationship or their actions consistently harm you emotionally or mentally, it's a sign that they may not have your best interests at heart.

Self-worth and Self-care: This mindset encourages self-respect. Understanding and honoring your worth makes you less likely to tolerate unhealthy or toxic relationships. You choose relationships that uplift and nurture you rather than those that deplete or harm you.

Authenticity in Relationships: Being around people who have your best interest at heart also ensures an authentic relationship. These people celebrate your successes, challenge you to be better, and are there for you in times of difficulty. They offer constructive criticism rather than destructive judgment.

Emotional Well-being: Relationships should promote your emotional health, not drain it. When someone consistently undermines you, disrespects you, or doesn't show empathy for your needs, it negatively impacts your mental and emotional well-being. This principle suggests it's important to distance yourself from individuals who cause more harm than good.

Personal Growth and Empowerment: The people who genuinely want the best for you will encourage you to grow, try new things, and achieve your goals. A relationship should contribute to your empowerment, not hold you back or keep you stagnant.

Accountability and Loyalty: Trusting people who have your best interest at heart means knowing they'll hold you accountable and support you when you fall. They aren't there just for the good times; they stick around when you need them the most.

The Benefits

Increased Happiness and Peace of Mind: When surrounded by people who genuinely care about you, relationships have less emotional turmoil and more contentment.

Mental Health: Positive relationships reduce stress and promote better mental health. In contrast, toxic relationships can lead to anxiety, depression, and burnout.

Focus on What Truly Matters: By letting go of relationships that drain you, you free up emotional space to cultivate the most important relationships to your happiness.

Reflection

Self-preservationism involves building a life and relationships in which you feel valued, supported, and motivated. By being selective and intentional about the people you let into your life, you ensure that the relationships you invest in are deserving of your time, energy, and love.

CHAPTER 2

Passionism - In life, there are many options, choose one and give it your all

Passionism requires us to choose a path. It means making genuine decisions, accepting the consequences, and actively engaging in life without depending on predetermined destinies or external validation.

The belief that life offers countless options, but true success lies in choosing one and giving it your all, addresses a common dilemma in our modern world: the paradox of choice. With infinite paths to explore, many people become paralyzed by indecision, fearing they may choose the wrong one. However, this philosophy reminds us that fulfillment rarely comes from perfect choices; instead, it emerges when we commit wholeheartedly to a single course of action.

I love all sports. However, I did not have the time to play all sports and needed to pick just one to focus on. I particularly love the sport of racquetball. Racquetball gets you in great physical shape, challenges you mentally, meets some great people, and allows you to release a great amount of stress. While playing, I don't think about my daily struggles, world problems, money, relationships, or anything else. I could play racquetball for hours, and that is how I knew it was my passion. When you find your passion, you don't think about it. Finding your passion is a pursuit where you are rewarded with a peaceful existence. Whether you find your passion in a hobby, a career, or any other interest, you will be rewarded with a great deal of peace.

The Modern Dilemma of Over-choice

Opportunities abound in today's world. Career paths have multiplied beyond traditional roles, and social connections span the globe. Information on hobbies, goals, and interests is just a click away. While abundant choice sounds like freedom, it often breeds anxiety.

Decision fatigue: The more options we face, the harder it becomes to decide. There's always a better option waiting around the corner. However, what truly matters is not the path you take but the commitment you bring to it.

The Pitfalls of Perpetual Searching

Fear of Missing Out (FOMO): Constantly wondering "what if?" prevents full engagement with the present.

Superficial Efforts: Trying a little bit of everything without investing in anything deeply leads to mediocrity.

Analysis Paralysis: Overthinking leads to inaction, leaving potential unrealized.

Why Commitment Matters

Momentum: Progress builds when you focus on one direction without constantly second-guessing yourself.
Mastery: Excellence requires sustained effort only when you stick with something long enough to improve.
Fulfillment: Deep engagement with a single pursuit often brings more satisfaction than dabbling in many.

Practical Wisdom: How to Choose and Commit

Start Where You Are: Don't wait for the perfect option—choose something practical and meaningful right now.
Silence Perfectionism: Understand that no choice is flawless. Growth happens along the way.
Set Boundaries on Exploration: Give yourself a reasonable timeframe to evaluate options, then choose one without looking back.
Reframe Failure: The lessons learned will remain valuable even if a choice doesn't yield the expected outcome.

The Magic of Giving It Your All

When you fully commit, unexpected doors open, and mastery creates new opportunities, connections, and breakthroughs that wouldn't have come from half-hearted efforts. By directing your energy, life often rewards you in ways that surpass initial expectations.

Reflection

Life isn't about waiting for the perfect path to reveal itself; it's about creating a meaningful journey on the path you select. There are many "right" choices in life, but none of them will matter unless you commit to them and give your all.

Just Do it-Doism

Doism is the concept of action without hesitation, fear, or overthinking. It's a philosophy rooted in the belief that the best way to approach life is by simply doing things, not waiting for the "perfect" moment or second-guessing oneself. Doism is about embracing action, learning through experience, and pushing forward with an unwavering commitment to progress. It emphasizes action over contemplation, focusing on the process of doing rather than dwelling on potential failure or obstacles.

In this context, it encourages overcoming fear by focusing entirely on the present task and taking action without getting bogged down by doubt. It's about embracing the moment and moving forward regardless of what may come.

I was often asked, "How did you get to where you are?" and "What do you do for a living?" I would smile and reply, "I never turned down any assignment." During my senior year, my classmates asked about my plans after graduation. I told them I was heading to Washington, DC, to work for the government. They wondered if I had a job, and I replied no. Then they asked if I had a place to stay, and once again, I said no. They couldn't believe I was choosing to go to Washington, DC, without a job or housing. But I confidently answered, "Yes."

After graduation, I packed everything I owned into a trailer, hitched it to my 12-year-old car, and drove to Washington, DC, with the $3,000 I had saved. I wasn't worried about the details; I was determined to make this happen and had faith in myself. I didn't have a Plan B.

At 22, I was naive about how things truly worked. Initially, I tried to sign a lease on an apartment, only to realize I needed a job first. I eventually found an apartment complex that offered month-to-month leases. At the same time, I secured a fast-food job while applying to various federal agencies in Washington, D.C. I didn't understand how challenging it could be to get employment with the federal government. I never contemplated the possibility of failure or not achieving my goal.

If you spend your time worrying about failure, you will never succeed. Negative thoughts about failure should never enter your mind. If you do fail, move on; don't dwell on it—focus on the next challenge instead. I've been told that not everyone has the mindset to "do it," but I disagree. Anyone can be a doer. You just need to take action and not fear failure. This mindset has served me well.

Looking back, I thought I was doing what anyone would do, and I didn't fully grasp the magnitude of this adventure. Yet, just three months after arriving in Washington, DC, I landed my dream job.

Action Over Contemplation

At its core, Doism stresses the importance of doing over endless deliberation. While planning and thinking are valuable, they shouldn't become obstacles to taking action. The philosophy encourages individuals to step forward without worrying about the outcome or potential failure.

Fearlessness

A central element of Doism is rejecting fear as a barrier to progress. Fear is seen as a natural feeling in this mindset, but it should never dictate your actions. Instead of pondering what might go wrong, Doism advocates pushing through fear and uncertainties with confidence and a sense of purpose.

Living in the Present

Doism encourages living in the moment. It encourages immersing yourself in the now, where action is the focus. Any distractions or overthinking about past failures or future uncertainties are minimized. The present is the only time you can act, so energy and attention should be concentrated there.

Embracing Growth Through Action

Instead of being paralyzed by the possibility of failure, Doism advocates for growth through experience. Failure isn't viewed as something negative but as a necessary part of learning. The more you do, the more you learn, refine, and grow—whether you succeed or not.

Resilience

The **Doism** mindset values resilience. It's not about succeeding immediately but persistently taking action, learning, and adjusting. Resilience is seen in the ability to keep moving forward despite setbacks, knowing that doing so leads to progress.

Minimalism in Thought

Overthinking can hinder progress. Doism promotes simplicity in thinking, eliminating unnecessary complexities and focusing only on what's essential for the task at hand. This can lead to more transparency, quicker decision-making, and more effective action.

The Benefits of Doism

Increased Productivity: Focusing on taking action instead of worrying about what might go wrong, individuals may become more productive and get more done.
Faster Learning: Through trial and error, you learn faster because you're actively engaging in the process rather than waiting for perfection.
Reduced Stress: Doism can reduce anxiety and stress without the weight of fear or excessive planning. Action brings clarity.
Self-Empowerment: Consistent choosing to do, despite fear, can build confidence, autonomy, and a strong sense of self-efficacy.

Examples of Doism in Action

Entrepreneurs: Many successful entrepreneurs embody **Doism**. Instead of waiting for the "perfect" business idea or fearing failure, they take action and launch their projects based on real-world feedback.

Artists and Creatives: For many creators, creating is more important than perfecting their work. They dive in, experiment, and evolve through doing rather than letting fear of imperfection hold them back.

Athletes: A mindset of action and resilience, where athletes push forward regardless of the odds, focusing on doing rather than worrying about failing or falling short.

Reflection

While Doism can effectively overcome barriers such as procrastination and fear, it is important to balance it with strategic thinking. An entirely unreflective approach may lead to poor decisions or burnout. Therefore, while Doism encourages action, it is also essential to dedicate time to rest and reflect when needed.

In summary, Doism focuses on harnessing the power of action, trusting the process, and not allowing fear, doubt, or overthinking to hold you back. It's a liberating philosophy that inspires living boldly and taking necessary actions, regardless of the uncertainties that may lie ahead.

Dogmatism - If there is any doubt, there is no doubt

Dogmatism is a rigid, unwavering belief in specific principles or doctrines, often leaving no room for doubt or questioning. In this mindset, doubt is seen as a sign that the belief is not fully established or definitive. However, doubt should not be regarded as incompatible with absolute certainty or conviction. Instead of dismissing doubt as a fleeting emotion, consider it a red flag; a signal that something isn't quite right, even if you can't immediately express why.

Several years ago, I was in the market to buy a house and had finally chosen a property. I negotiated the price, made a down payment, and set a closing date. About three weeks into the contract period, I began to have doubts about the purchase. Unsure why I felt this way, I spoke to the realtor. She explained that I would lose my earnest money if I decided to back out of the purchase. My doubts lingered for another week, and ultimately, I chose to walk away from the deal, forfeiting my earnest money. Once I made that decision, I no longer had any doubts. This confirmed that I had made the right choice in canceling the purchase. In summary, my initial doubts about the house led me to cancel the purchase, and my certainty afterward affirmed that I had made the right decision.

The Nature of Doubt

Doubt arises when information or instincts clash with expectations or desires. It may manifest as a subtle unease, an unanswered question, or a gut feeling that refuses to be ignored. While doubt doesn't always mean disaster, it often signals that clarity or certainty is lacking.

Practical Interpretations

Intuition as Intelligence: The brain processes vast amounts of information subconsciously. Doubt maybe your mind's way of flagging something you haven't consciously identified yet.
Risk Management: In high-stakes environments (such as

military operations or financial decisions), caution can prevent costly mistakes when doubt appears.

Personal Boundaries: Doubt often signals in relationships that trust, compatibility, or communication may be lacking and need attention.

Applications in Everyday Life

Business Decisions: If you're uncertain about a potential partnership or investment, investigate further or wait for clarity.

Relationships: When doubt clouds your judgment about someone's intentions, that doubt itself may be revealing something important.

Creative Endeavors: When you're not fully committed to an idea or project, doubt often reflects a lack of passion or readiness.

Safety and Security: This principle is often used in self-defense: If a situation feels wrong, trust your gut and leave it.

The Shadow Side of This "Ism"

While trusting doubt can be wise, excessive reliance may breed indecisiveness or paranoia. Not all doubts are deal-breakers; some are natural parts of growth and learning. Doubt can spiral into endless questioning and prevent action. Unchecked doubt may lead to missed opportunities.

Balancing Doubt with Discernment

Context Matters: Is the doubt rooted in fear, unfamiliarity, or actual risk?

Seek Information: When possible, gather facts to address doubts rather than dismissing them outright.

Consult Others: Talking through your doubts with trusted advisors can provide clarity.

Trust Your Gut but Verify: Use intuition as a guide, not the final word.

Reflection

When doubt arises, it often serves a purpose. It may signal danger, indicate a lack of preparation, or simply suggest a need for reflection. Listening to that inner voice can save us time, heartache, and resources. Life rewards those who act decisively but think carefully; this approach empowers us to navigate that delicate balance.

CHAPTER 3

Goodism - Don't engage in any transaction that you didn't initiate

Goodism suggests avoiding deals or transactions that you didn't initiate, as they may lead to mistakes in areas like finances or scams. It emphasizes the importance of maintaining control over your financial decisions and being vigilant when approached by unsolicited offers or opportunities, whether online, over the phone, or in person.

I learned this lesson when I was about 16 years old and went to the mall to buy some shoes. A stranger struck up a conversation with me outside the mall and asked what I was planning to buy. When I mentioned the shoes, he advised against purchasing them there. He claimed to have a friend who sold the same shoes for a fraction of the cost. When I asked, "What? Where is he?" he offered to take me to him. In the end, he led me all over the city and stole all my money. I didn't buy any shoes that day, but I learned a valuable lesson.

Another experience involved a friend who suggested I consider buying a timeshare. I had never thought about it before and initially agreed to consider it. Ultimately, I decided against it, as I didn't want or need a timeshare. When I told my friend about my decision, he became upset and eventually ended our long friendship. Now, when faced with similar offers, I simply say I am not interested. Today, you cannot sell me anything I did not intend to purchase. I also avoid engaging with people through spam or scam emails and texts on Facebook and other social media platforms. This approach saves me both money and emotional distress.

Why It Matters

In today's fast-paced digital world, scams are becoming more sophisticated. From phishing emails to fraudulent investment schemes, malicious actors often use deception to catch unsuspecting individuals off guard. A common tactic they use is creating a sense of urgency with offers that seem "too good to be true." To protect yourself, remember that you should only pay attention to offers if you initiated the contact.

Financial Wisdom

Focusing solely on transactions that you control is essential for maintaining financial discipline. By proactively seeking out opportunities instead of reacting impulsively to unsolicited offers, you allow yourself the time to conduct thorough research, compare options, and make decisions based on logic rather than emotion. This approach reduces the likelihood of impulsive spending, risky investments, and unnecessary financial risks.

Scam Prevention

This principle serves as a safeguard against scams that thrive on manipulation, such as:

Phishing Emails: Fraudulent messages designed to steal sensitive information by prompting action.

Investment Schemes: "Hot tip" opportunities promising unrealistically high returns.

Unexpected Calls or Texts: Scammers pretending to represent legitimate companies requesting payments or information.

Imposter Scams: Posing as friends, family, or authority figures asking for financial help.

Reflection

By refusing to engage in unsolicited transactions, you protect yourself from fraudulent tactics. Genuine opportunities rarely appear out of the blue; they typically require effort, research, and intentional pursuit. By initiating transactions yourself, you can avoid becoming entangled in the agendas or demands of others, ensuring that your actions are intentional and beneficial to you.

In summary, the advice to avoid transactions you did not initiate highlights the need for control, practicality, and purposeful action. This approach encourages a mindset where you make proactive choices that align with your goals, minimize unnecessary risks, and focus your time and energy on actions that lead to beneficial results. It's about taking responsibility for your decisions and engaging only in activities that support your long-term success and well-being.

Egoism - You have always to do what is best for you. No one else will put you first

Egoism emphasizes the importance of individuals acting in their own best interest. At its core, it asserts that you are primarily responsible for your own well-being and success. No one else is guaranteed to prioritize your needs as much as you do.

I learned the importance of this when a friend asked me for a cash loan. He assured me that he would repay me within a specific timeframe. When the repayment date arrived, my friend had several excuses. One of his reasons was that I didn't really need the money since I wouldn't have lent it to him if I did. I was appalled by this reasoning. As a result of prioritizing my friend, I found myself in unnecessary hardship. From that moment on, I decided never to "loan" money to anyone again. If I decide to help someone in need, I do so without expectation.

Workplace Boundaries

Imagine an employee who constantly volunteers for extra projects, even if it means sacrificing their own responsibilities. Over time, they become overworked and stressed while their efforts go unnoticed. Once they learn to say "no" to tasks that don't align with their goals, they preserve their energy and earn the respect and recognition they deserve.

Healthy Relationships

Consider someone in a relationship who routinely puts

their partner's needs ahead of their own. They might cancel personal plans, ignore their hobbies, or suppress their feelings to maintain peace. Eventually, this person may feel resentful and drained. By setting healthy boundaries and prioritizing their own emotional well-being, they can create a more balanced and fulfilling relationship.

Financial Self-Care

Think of someone who always agrees to lend money or cover expenses for friends and family, even when it strains their own budget. Over time, they may struggle financially because they never save or invest in their future. Learning to prioritize personal financial health—such as saying "no" to unsustainable spending—helps them build security and achieve long-term goals.

Personal Health

A caregiver or parent who neglects their own well-being to cater to everyone else's needs can quickly burn out. By scheduling regular time for exercise, relaxation, and hobbies, they not only improve their health but also become better equipped to support others sustainably.

Academic Prioritization

Consider a student who is always the go-to person for group assignments and tutoring their peers, leaving little time for their own studying and rest. When they learn to set boundaries and allocate dedicated time for their learning, they often see a marked improvement in their academic performance and overall well-being.

Reflection

Egoism is not selfishness; it is a recognition that your well-being is the basis for everything you do. You honor your needs, aspirations, and boundaries by putting yourself first. No one else is obligated to champion your interests or protect your energy; it is essential that you become your greatest advocate. Embracing egoism means understanding that true fulfillment and the strength to support others begin with taking care of yourself. Ultimately, prioritizing what is best for you fosters a resilient and empowered self, capable of navigating life's challenges with confidence and clarity.

Realism - Not everyone is going to get on the train

Realism acknowledges the harsh truth that not everyone will succeed, not everyone will "get on the train" of progress, and not everyone will achieve the same goals. It suggests that reality is often unfair and unequal and that individuals encounter various circumstances, opportunities, and paths in life. Realism recognizes that, despite our best efforts, some people will be left behind, which is an inevitable part of life, and that's perfectly okay.

I learned about this dynamic during my time as a supervisor. As a strong advocate for teamwork, I frequently organized team-building events during work hours. All expenses were covered, and the activities were meant to be enjoyable.

However, I often encountered employees who declined to participate. A specific reason was rarely given, and I was even asked if attendance was required. I struggled to understand why anyone would refuse an opportunity to connect with their teammates on company time, especially since it was free of charge.

After reflecting on this, I decided to clarify the situation: participation in the team-building exercises was not mandatory; however, if someone chose to opt out, their non-participation would be noted in their annual performance reviews. At that moment, I realized that not everyone was interested in being part of the team. Some individuals simply did not care about building relationships with their colleagues or contributing to the organization's success.

From then on, when I encountered someone unwilling to engage, I accepted that the train would leave without them. As a result, those who stood on the platform while the train departed eventually found themselves behind in promotions, bonuses, and significant assignments.

Life presents countless paths, each requiring decisions about direction, companions, and priorities. As we embark on "trains" to new destinations—whether it be a career change, personal growth, or new relationships—it's inevitable that some people will be left behind.

Different Destinations

People have their own dreams and life goals. Not everyone will align with your path. Some people resist growth or are uncomfortable with others evolving because it disrupts the status quo. Friendships, relationships, and collaborations may be meaningful in one phase of life but naturally fade as circumstances change.

Why This Matters

Letting Go of Expectations: Holding on to the idea that everyone must support or join your journey creates unnecessary frustration.

Avoiding Resentment: Acceptance allows you to appreciate past connections without bitterness when they don't continue forward.

Focusing on Alignment: Surrounding yourself with people who share your vision or growth mindset fuels progress and fulfillment.

Practical Wisdom

Don't Wait at the Station: If someone hesitates or refuses to support your path, don't stall your progress, hoping they'll change their mind.
Be Grateful for Past Passengers: Acknowledge the positive influence of those who were once part of your journey, even if they don't remain.
Seek New Passengers: Life introduces new people aligned with your evolving self—mentors, friends, and partners who fit your current path.
Trust the Process: Just because someone isn't on your train now doesn't mean they never will be. Paths may reconnect in the future.

Reflection

Not everyone is meant to travel with you on your journey, and that is perfectly natural. Some people come into your life to teach you lessons, share laughter, or walk beside you for a season. However, they may choose to stay behind when you embark on a new chapter.

By accepting this truth, you free yourself from unnecessary guilt, honor the beauty of change, and create space for meaningful connections that support your continued growth.

Cynicism - Trust, like the soul, once it is gone, it never returns
Latin Translation: Fide, ut anima semel profecta est, numquam redit.

Cynicism involves distrusting others' motives, particularly in relation to human sincerity and morality. It highlights that once trust is broken, restoring it can be complicated, if not impossible. A cynic believes that people primarily act in their self-interest, and when trust is lost, it rarely returns to its original state, much like how a soul cannot be fully "reclaimed" once it is gone.

I was in a relationship that had the potential to lead to marriage. After a year of dating, I made two specific requests to my partner: (1) that we not discuss our intimate moments with others, and (2) that she work on reducing her credit card balances. To help cut back on spending, we agreed that I would hold her credit cards and that we would use only cash for future purchases.

However, I soon discovered that our intimate moments were being discussed with others, and the credit card balances continued rising because my partner would go shopping and tell retailers that she had forgotten her credit card. Upon learning that my two requests were not only ignored but that there was also deception regarding the credit cards, my trust was shattered, and the relationship ended.

Several years later, we chose to meet again. Our meeting was cordial, and we talked for quite a while. However, the intense connection we once shared was no longer present. Essentially, the trust I had in her was gone. That trust had been the unifying and essential element of our relationship. Without it, we lacked a strong bond and could not regain what we had before. That was the last time I saw my former partner. Recognizing that broken trust cannot be repaired is a liberating truth. While relationships may end, self-awareness and personal growth endure.

Trust: The Fragile Foundation of Relationships

Trust is the invisible glue that holds relationships, institutions, and societies together. It represents the belief that others will act with honesty and integrity, even when unobserved. However, trust is earned over time through consistent actions, mutual respect, and authenticity. Once broken, repairing it becomes one of life's most significant challenges.

The damage of lost trust often feels permanent. Betrayal leads to hurt and uncertainty, making individuals question their judgment. Rebuilding trust requires much more effort than it took to earn it initially.

Think of a shattered vase: while it can be glued back together, the cracks are still visible. Similarly, relationships can be mended after a betrayal but often carry lingering doubts and scars. Trust is crucial for human connection, and while it can sometimes be rebuilt through sincere remorse and transparent behavior, it's easier to prevent trust from being lost than to repair it afterward.

Trust is essential in our complex world. Once lost, it rarely returns, leaving a void of doubt and skepticism. A betrayal —whether from a friend, partner, or leader—creates wounds that are difficult to heal, and while apologies may follow, the purity of the original trust is often gone.

Reflection

Cynicism disregards societal norms and conventional values, leading individuals to perceive the world with distrust and disillusionment. Cynics contend that people are often driven by self-interest, rendering the quest for external approval fundamentally unfulfilling.

Cynicism engenders a cautious approach to vulnerability; trusting others carries the risk of harm. It encourages emotional self-sufficiency and promotes skepticism when extending trust, implying that safety resides in self-reliance, particularly since many relationships can be flawed or transactional.

Trust demands continuous nurturing in both personal and societal contexts. A single misstep can destroy what took years to establish. Therefore, it's essential for individuals and institutions to prioritize the preservation of trust, understanding that its true value manifests in the destruction wrought by its absence.

CHAPTER 4

**Asceticism - To achieve anything, you must make
sacrifices**

Asceticism is the disciplined practice of renouncing worldly pleasures and comforts to achieve spiritual, intellectual, or personal growth. When we relate this philosophy to the notion that "to achieve anything, you must make sacrifices," asceticism becomes a guiding principle for intentional self-discipline and focus.

While asceticism is frequently associated with religious or spiritual practices, it also represents a broader perspective that attaining something meaningful requires sacrifices of time, energy, or personal comforts.

When I was 22, I learned a valuable lesson about life. After moving into an apartment, I found myself with no money for furniture, dishes, or any essentials. I ended up sleeping on the floor and created a strict budget. To save money, I stopped eating out and avoided spending on movies, clubs, and other forms of entertainment. Each month, I managed to save a little, and when I had enough, I bought one piece of furniture at a time.

Meanwhile, my friends were going into debt to furnish their homes and enjoy various activities. In the end, their debt cost them far more than the sacrifices I made. I learned that making sacrifices early on can lead to significant rewards later. In other words, I chose to delay immediate gratification from purchases to achieve greater satisfaction in the future.

Delayed Gratification

Immediate pleasures often distract from long-term goals. We invest in our future selves by willingly postponing gratification—whether that means forgoing leisure, luxury, or superficial indulgences. This self-denial is not about deprivation for its own sake; it's about clearing the path for **more** profound achievement and fulfillment.

Focus on Higher Purpose

Every sacrifice must be intentional and aligned with a higher purpose. This might mean sacrificing time, comfort, or material wealth to hone a craft, advance a career, or develop inner wisdom. The idea is to remove extraneous influences such as cloud judgment, allowing you to devote your energy fully to your pursuits.

Cultivation of Self-Discipline

Whether adhering to a strict routine, limiting social distractions, or maintaining a minimalistic lifestyle, these habits build resilience and sharpen focus. Over time, this disciplined approach becomes a powerful tool for personal transformation.

Embracing the Cost of Growth

The philosophy reminds us that nothing truly worthwhile is achieved without some form of sacrifice. Ascetics understand that every gain—skill, knowledge, or success—comes with a price. Accepting this cost is a cornerstone of the mindset: the hardships and sacrifices of today pave the way for the accomplishments of tomorrow.

Personal Development

A student who spends evenings studying instead of indulging in leisure activities practices asceticism. The sacrifice of immediate fun is an investment in future expertise and career success.

Artistic Mastery

Consider a musician or writer who commits to daily practice despite the lure of distractions. Their choice to sacrifice social outings and idle time cultivates a mastery that eventually sets them apart in their field.

Athletic Achievement

Athletes often adhere to rigorous training schedules, strict diets, and disciplined recovery routines. The ascetic commitment to sacrificing comfort and immediate pleasure leads to peak performance and long-term competitive success.

Entrepreneurship

Many successful entrepreneurs embrace a minimalist approach in the early stages of their ventures, sacrificing luxuries and immediate gratification to focus on building their business. Their disciplined approach helps them navigate challenges and secure long-term growth.

Reflection

When viewed through the lens of achievement, asceticism is not about self-imposed misery or unnecessary deprivation. Instead, it represents a conscious and empowering choice to invest in one's highest potential. Individuals create space for lasting success and personal growth by sacrificing temporary pleasures and distractions. Every significant achievement requires a trade-off. What you forgo today becomes the foundation for what you can build tomorrow.

ALTRUISM - Don't let money or power drive your pursuits

Altruism is the belief in or practice of caring selflessly for the well-being of others. It emphasizes prioritizing the welfare of others over the pursuit of personal wealth, power, or material gain. In this perspective, the endless chase for money or power is viewed as unfulfilling; true satisfaction comes from helping others and contributing to the greater good.

This perspective offers a timeless reminder about the emptiness of pursuing material wealth and influence as the ultimate goals. It encourages reflection on what truly brings fulfillment and warns against the relentless cycle of "more" that often consumes those who prioritize external markers of success.

One day, I arrived at work feeling happy and upbeat, just like usual. Later that day, I discovered that I was being removed from my position. As a result, I would no longer be earning the same amount of money or holding the same level of power that came with my role. Suddenly, I found myself in a depressed state of mind. I was in a funk, and my joy had vanished.

I began to realize that my depression stemmed from associating my happiness with money and power. This made me reflect on why I found joy in such superficial things. It was eye-opening to understand that money and power can come and go so easily. Throughout my healing process, which took time, I made a decision: I would never again tie my happiness or mental well-being to money or power.

Eventually, I secured a position that granted me authority and a higher income. However, this time, I did not define myself by the money or power associated with my role. I understood my own worth and recognized that money and power were just part of the job. As a result, I have never been happier.

The Insatiable Nature of Money and Power

Human beings adapt quickly to new levels of wealth or influence, craving more just to maintain the same satisfaction.
A pay raise initially feels exciting but soon becomes the norm, prompting the desire for another increase.
Climbing the ranks to a position of authority often leads to ambition for even more influence.

No Finish Line

Unlike goals grounded in creativity, purpose, or service, pursuing money and power lacks a clear endpoint.

Someone wealthier, more powerful, or seemingly "ahead" will always be on the path of life. The comparison trap ensures that satisfaction remains elusive.

The Cost of Money- and Power-Driven Pursuits
Personal Sacrifice

Prioritizing money or power can damage relationships, health, and mental well-being.

Erosion of Integrity

Ethical considerations often fall by the wayside when the focus becomes solely on climbing higher.

Loneliness at the Top

Obsession with control or wealth can isolate individuals from genuine human connections.

Shifting the Measure of Success

Instead of allowing money or power to dictate pursuits, this "ism" encourages a focus on values and pursuits that foster meaning, fulfillment, and connection.

Purpose

Pursue work and goals aligned with your values and passions.

Impact

Seek to contribute positively to the lives of others.

Personal Growth

Strive to become a better version of yourself rather than amassing material possessions.

Financial Decisions

Instead of endlessly chasing higher income, focus on achieving financial freedom that supports a meaningful life.

Career Choices

Seek roles that offer growth, satisfaction, and purpose, not just prestige or higher pay.

Daily Life

Measure success by quality relationships, joy in small moments, and alignment with personal values.

Reflection

While money and power can provide temporary satisfaction, they are inadequate substitutes for lasting happiness. By prioritizing purpose, relationships, and personal growth, life becomes richer, not in material wealth, but in fulfillment and meaning.

Optimism - Get busy living or get busy dying

Life seldom offers a middle ground. Optimism requires moving forward, engaging with the world, and embracing the struggle. Otherwise, you gradually slip into apathy, allowing time to take its toll. The phrase popularized in The Shawshank Redemption is more than just a memorable movie quote; it serves as a call to action—a clear choice between embracing life with all its uncertainties or surrendering to the slow decay of indifference.

Growing up in an inner city, I was surrounded by crime and violence every day, which left me feeling apathetic. My first year of high school exposed me to a culture of negativity, and I even witnessed people getting shot inside the building. At the time, I didn't realize how much I was suffering emotionally and intellectually. I attended my classes but didn't complete any assignments or participate in discussions. I would just sit in my assigned seat and zone out. One of my teachers told me that since I wasn't doing anything, I deserved an "F," but she would give me a "D" instead. By the end of my freshman year, my overall grade point average was a "D."

During the summer between my first and second years, I continued to witness friends passing away. I quickly realized that if I stayed on this path, I would also end up dead. That's when I decided to get busy living instead of getting busy dying. After making that choice, I felt the weight of dread I had been carrying lift. From my sophomore year through graduation, I participated in sports and graduated with the fifth-highest GPA in my class of 400. I have maintained my mantra of getting busy living and savoring every moment.

The Paralysis of Apathy

Apathy is a silent thief. It doesn't break down the door; instead, it seeps through the cracks, settling into the spaces where purpose once existed. People who feel lost and wake up each day without a sense of direction often don't consciously decide to give up; instead, they simply stop choosing to engage. The weight of depression and the feeling of disconnection from meaning can make even the simplest acts of living feel unbearably heavy.

For those who have lost their way, life becomes a passive existence. Days blend into one another, and the mind becomes clouded with disinterest. Ambitions diminish, relationships fade, and an invisible barrier grows between them and the world around them. They aren't necessarily choosing to die, but they aren't choosing to live, either.

Hopelessness

Hopelessness is a poison that turns possibilities into dead ends. Those trapped in despair see the future as a wasteland —barren and devoid of opportunity. Why bother trying when nothing seems to matter? Why move forward when the weight of existence feels so heavy? Negative thoughts whisper: It's too late. You've failed. No one cares.

However, these are illusions. When overwhelmed by negativity, the mind can fabricate lies. Hope is still a spark waiting to be rekindled, even in its faintest form. The possibility of transformation becomes real when a person recognizes that they can choose differently and starts to actively engage in life.

The Value of Living

To get busy living means embracing life in all its messiness. It doesn't imply constant happiness, nor does it require grand gestures. It means waking up each day and deciding to participate.

Finding Purpose

Purpose isn't always about world-changing ambitions. It can be found in the small things: creating, learning, helping someone else, or simply committing to growth.

Seeking Connection

Isolation feeds apathy, while human connection sparks vitality. Engaging in conversations, seeking out friendships, or being present with loved ones can reignite the sense of belonging.

Pursuing Curiosity

Life thrives on discovery. Whether exploring new ideas, traveling to unfamiliar places, or simply opening oneself up to new experiences, curiosity is a fuel that keeps the spirit engaged.

Embracing the Struggle

To live is to struggle, but struggle isn't synonymous with failure. It's the process of becoming. The challenges, setbacks, and moments of doubt are not signs of defeat but growth markers.

Reflection

Each day presents the same question: Will you get busy living, or will you get busy dying? There is no neutral ground. Even inaction is a choice. For those who have felt lost or hopeless, remember this: living is always an option. It requires effort and courage, but it is always worth it. Sometimes, the first step to getting busy living is simply deciding to try.

To "get busy living" means to continue making choices that bring fulfillment in the present, despite the fact that life will never offer absolute answers. Ultimately, this phrase reminds us that life, with all its chaos and meaninglessness, is a gift if we choose to embrace it. Whether we find our purpose in small acts of kindness, the pursuit of personal goals, or simply by accepting the absurdity of life with humor.

Pragmatism - Live for today with the future in mind

Pragmatism approaches problems and decisions based on real-world outcomes. It also involves making choices that work now and, in the long run, focusing on balance and adaptability.

Health

Being mindful of present health choices (e.g., diet, exercise) while considering their long-term effects on well-being.

Finances

Balancing the enjoyment of current spending with the foresight to save and plan for future financial stability.

Relationships

Cultivating meaningful connections today while nurturing those relationships to ensure they thrive in the future.

I recall a coworker who believed that saving every penny was the best way to manage money. Although we received extra funds for meals and travel, known as per diem, he would skip meals to use the entire per diem money to pay down the principal on his mortgage. While I thought his strategy wasn't bad, I felt he was neglecting the present by focusing solely on the future. I couldn't see myself concentrating only on what's ahead, especially when the future is uncertain for everyone. Instead, I preferred to enjoy good meals while continuing to save my regular income for what lies ahead.

Balanced Living

A delicate balance exists between enjoying the present and preparing for the future. We need to fully engage with life today while making wise choices that protect and enhance tomorrow.

Living for Today

Enjoy an active, vibrant lifestyle. Savor good food, exercise regularly, and prioritize mental well-being. Your body deserves care and enjoyment now, not just in your retirement years.

Keeping the Future in Mind

Avoid destructive habits and proactively approach long-term health. Regular checkups, balanced nutrition, and preventive care reduce the risk of chronic diseases.

Finances: Balance Spending and Saving

Enjoy what you earn by treating yourself to experiences, hobbies, and occasional splurges. Don't delay all happiness for "someday."

Relationships: Cultivate Bonds That Last

Show appreciation, spend quality time, and create lasting memories with loved ones. Don't take relationships for granted.

BUILD TRUST, understanding, and forgiveness. Strong relationships require care and effort over time.

Reflection

"Live for today with the future in mind" encourages us to embrace the present while considering the long-term impact of our choices, advocating for a balanced approach to living.

Sameism - Women/Men may be different, but we are the same

Despite the apparent differences between men and women, people fundamentally share universal desires, wants, and needs.

I recently overheard a 9-year-old girl in Naples, Italy, talking with her mother. The mother wanted her to visit the Pompeii Ruins, but the girl insisted she didn't want to, saying she had seen plenty of ruins. The mother claimed these were different, to which the girl replied, "They may be different, but they are still ruins." I was impressed by her understanding of a complex idea. Eventually, it seemed they did not go to the Pompei ruins.

This interaction reminded me of how people talk about relationships. My friends often mention a new partner, saying, "Oh, she's different; she likes this and that." I respond, "Yes, she may be different, but she's still the same as all women."

Although men and women belong to different gender categories, they share similar needs and desires. For example, when a man's relationship ends and someone asks why, he lists reasons that often repeat in his new relationship. Six months later, if asked how it's going, he might say, "Not so good," and he realizes the new partner has traits resembling those of his previous partners. After some reflection, he often agrees, saying, "You're right; they may be different women, but they're all still women."

Full disclosure: This ism does not pertain to abusive,

criminal, or deviant behavior. **No amount of abuse is acceptable in any relationship and should end that relationship, period.**

Desires

At a fundamental level, both women and men desire love, respect, purpose, and fulfillment. Although society often portrays these desires differently—suggesting that women seek emotional intimacy while men focus on ambition—the reality is that these impulses overlap. Everyone, regardless of gender, wants to be seen, heard, and valued.

Societal expectations can pressure women to seek validation through relationships and men through achievements. However, when we remove these external pressures, it becomes clear that both groups are searching for a sense of meaning and connection.

Wants

Wants are more specific and influenced by culture, yet they are similar across genders. The difference often lies not in what people want but rather in how they prioritize these desires due to societal conditioning.

Career success

Both men and women increasingly pursue professional growth and autonomy.

Family life

While traditional norms once positioned women as the primary caregivers, the evolving modern landscape reveals a shared desire for fulfilling family bonds.

Recognition

Everyone seeks acknowledgment for their contributions and talents.

Needs

At a deeper level, our human needs are universally the same. Despite their differences in expression, women and men share the same fundamental human requirements.

Physiological - Food, water, shelter.

Safety - Security, health, stability.

Love and belonging - Intimacy and community.

Esteem - Confidence, respect, and recognition.

Self-actualization - Realizing one's potential

Reflection

Sameism conveys the notion that unity and shared experiences bind us together, even amid our superficial differences. We all have similar needs, desires, emotions, and experiences, regardless of our cultures, genders, races, or beliefs. In a world frequently marked by division and conflict, Sameism inspires us to recognize our common humanity and to celebrate our differences as a form of diversity rather than as grounds for discord. It fosters empathy and understanding, helping us to discern the deeper truths that unite us.

FINAL REFLECTION

Final Reflection

If you've reached this point, you've done more than read about isms; you've confronted them. You've walked through the quiet spaces where beliefs are born and the noisy crossroads where they're questioned. You've explored the ideas that shape you. Some you've inherited, some you've chosen, and others you've carried unknowingly, simply because the world expected you to.

Maybe a few chapters made you nod in agreement. Maybe others made you pause, uncomfortable with the truth they revealed. That's how awareness works; it doesn't ask for permission. It shows up when you're ready.

This novella wasn't written to give you rules or resolutions. It was written to remind you that you are not powerless in a world full of noise and motion. You are not just reacting to life; you are shaping it every single day through what you believe, what you challenge, what you let go of, and what you decide to hold tight.

The isms in your life don't define you; you define them.

As I have defined the isms based on my personal beliefs and experiences, you can choose which ones empower you and hold you back. Which ones align with who you are becoming and no longer fit the life you're creating?

So take what speaks to you. Question what doesn't. Start conversations. Redraw boundaries. Be open to change but firm in your values. And when the world feels off-kilter again, it inevitably will return to these pages. Revisit these isms. See how they've shifted. See how *you've* shifted.

Because growth isn't always loud, sometimes, it's in the quiet decision to see more clearly, to choose more intentionally, and to live more freely. And if nothing else stays with you, let this truth echo long after the final page.

You are allowed to evolve. You are allowed to question. You are allowed to grow beyond the isms that no longer serve you. The power was never in the isms. It was always in you.

Let's go...and live our Best Lives

www.ingramcontent.com/pod-product-compliance
Lightning Source LLC
Chambersburg PA
CBHW071542120626
46550CB00006B/2553